ANDREA JAMES is a Yorta Yorta/Kurnai woman and graduate of VCA. She was Artistic Director of Melbourne Workers' Theatre 2001–2008 where she is best known for her play *Yanagai! Yanagai!*. Relocating to Sydney, Andrea was the Aboriginal Arts Development Officer at Blacktown Arts Centre 2010–2012 and Aboriginal Producer at Carriageworks from 2012–2016 and is currently part-time Blak Box Producer for Urban Theatre Projects.

She was a recipient of British Council's Accelerate Program for Aboriginal Art Leaders in 2013 and was awarded an Arts NSW Aboriginal Arts Fellowship to write a play about Wiradjuri tennis player, Evonne Goolagong. Andrea performed in and co-wrote *Bright World* with Elise Hearst for Arthur Productions at Theatreworks in April 2015. She directed her play *Winyanboga Yurringa* at Carriageworks and Geelong Performing Arts Centre in August 2016. *Winyanboga Yurringa* is being remounted by Belvoir in May 2019. Her short play, *Blacktown Angels*, premiered at Sydney Festival in 2016 for Urban Theatre Project's *Home Country*. She was a collaborator in Moogahlin Performing Arts *Broken Glass* which she performed in at the Sydney Festival in 2017. In 2018 she wrote and directed a play entitled *Bukal* for JUTE Theatre that tells the inspirational story of Yidinji woman Henrietta Fourmile Marrie.

Alexis Lane as Chantelle in the Moogahlin Performing Arts production in 2016. (Photo: Michele Mossop)

WINYANBOGA YURRINGA

ANDREA JAMES

CURRENCY PRESS
The performing arts publisher

CURRENCY PLAYS

First published in 2019
by Currency Press Pty Ltd,
PO Box 2287, Strawberry Hills, NSW, 2012, Australia
enquiries@currency.com.au
www.currency.com.au

Typeset by Dean Nottle for Currency Press.
Cover design and illustration by Lisa White for Currency Press.

A catalogue record for this book is available from the National Library of Australia

Contents

Currency Press acknowledges the Traditional Owners of the Country on which we live and work. We pay our respects to all Aboriginal and Torres Strait Islander Elders, past and present.

*For Dayna James-French,
my little Woman of the Sun*

Left to right: Alexis Lane as Chantelle, Kylie Coolwell as Margie, Pamela Young as Carol, and Angeline Penrith as Wanda in the Moogahlin Performing Arts production in 2016. (Photo: Michele Mossop)

GANBINA!

There, on the first dawn, before time
The mind was pure sustenance
   Born long ago
   Before body
It moved freely, yet with purpose
It knows boundless space
    Having come from there
It spans this web of the universe
    From which the planets hang suspended
    Every turning
    Stars glittering in the velvet darkness of forever
The sun, through it, is giver of warm life
The rain (from that same source it comes)
    Messenger of Life
Wind is its voice, telling the earth always of Life

Hyllus Maris

Inspired by the critically acclaimed and award-winning TV series of 1983, *Women of the Sun*, *Winyanboga Yurringa* pays honour and tribute to the writers, Yorta Yorta Elder Hyllus Maris (1933–1986) and Sonia Borg. A formidable writing team, Maris and Borg championed the women's voices within the recent history of Indigenous Australia to be heard, shared and absorbed at a time when Indigenous peoples, especially Indigenous women's experiences, were not a part of the vernacular, nor seen as vital to the Australian storytelling landscape. Writer and director Andrea James, referencing the characters Towradgi and Wonda, captures the essence of *Women of the Sun* by continuing the storytelling traditions of the Yorta Yorta and bringing the storied narratives to the present.

Growing up in the '70s and '80s in Echuca on Yorta Yorta country, hearing the stories and attitudes in school about the 'aborigines' of the area were very different to the stories that were told at home. Classroom stories always left me feeling frustrated, angry, ashamed, lesser than my fellow classmates and even fearful of my own kin. My classmates would say things like, 'You're not like the coons from Cummera, you're like us!'

It always perplexed me as to this distinction, why they chose to discriminate against my family and community and why there was such a need to 'claim' me as one of 'their' own. Of course, I was no different to my mob out at Cummera, though I did feel the impact of narratives that attempted to separate me from my own on a daily basis.

At the time I didn't have the language to tell the class how I was more like the Cummera mob than them or to express my pride in being Yorta Yorta Dja Dja Wurrung. So, it became a lifetime commitment to seek the language and expressions of other like-minded black fullas who could speak this truth and pride of who they were and who we are. James is one of those souls who has experienced a similar devaluing. We are Yorta Yorta and our Ancestors' blood runs through our veins, their ideas, ways of being and philosophies are imbedded in our psyche, our breath, our heartbeats.

Being listened to and heard are things we all need. Judgement and fear of difference have held many in the grip of fear for lifetimes, silencing voices with stories that are the very threads of our society and culture. It is here in *Winyanboga Yurringa* that we see the breaking of this colonial violence: we are not one nation, we are not the same, with diverse views in a world where we are forced to constantly navigate colonialism. We are not a one-dimensional people; we are complex characters with different ideas about the world and how we are able to be in that world. *Winyanboga Yurringa* explores these issues, transporting audiences to a deeper place of understanding by positioning Indigenous women as the foci.

Funny, raw, real Koori women, *Winyanboga Yurringa* speaks truths, our truths, our realities. James has created characters that have integrity and resilience, including woka (country) as a character with agency and speaking in her own voice.

The language is valid, this is the way we speak with each other—loving, harsh, insensitive, gentle, honest, cutting, truthful, gammin, kind, nurturing.

Winyanboga Yurringa has succeeded in representing true characters heightened by the theatrical experience. The fears and frustrations, the love and the humour are ingredients of our complex lives and *Winyanboga Yurringa* makes that extremely clear, singing it from the tops of the Dharnya and down the mighty Dhungala, the message flows.

It is always refreshing and relieving to hear our stories illuminated in the theatre space by Indigenous writers and storytellers. *Winyanboga Yurringa* challenges the hegemonic stories that have been created out of fantastical tales of settler tropes that continue to haunt the very stages we now inhabit, however, there is no stopping our stories now. There is a rise, a call to respond to the old voices on the wind, to continue telling, speaking, singing and dancing—we follow in the footsteps of our dhama yenbena, our old people, we do not stand on our Ancestors' shoulders— we walk beside each other in strength, solidarity and sovereignty.

Yorta Yorta woka deyawin, murrangurang!

Dr Lou Bennett AM

Dr Lou Bennett AM is Yorta Yorta Dja Dja Wurrung. Dr Bennett is an artist and academic of 30 years, working in the field of Indigenous language retrieval. Her research project is called 'Sovereign Language Rematriation Through Song Pedagogy'.

AUTHOR'S NOTE

Winyanboga Yurringa was commissioned by Belvoir Theatre in January 2010 as part of an ambitious theatre project to create a stage adaptation of Hyllus Maris and Sonia Borg's iconic 'Women of the Sun' that was also made into a tele-series for SBS-TV directed by Bob Weiss. The project was guided and co-written by Tony Briggs (Auntie Hyllus's nephew) and directed/co-written by Wesley Enoch with fellow writers Romaine Moreton, Alana Valentine and Stephen Page who each adapted an episode of the story. My task was to write a 'new episode' with the leading question, 'Who is our Woman of the Sun today and what are her major concerns?' And thus, *Winyanboga Yurringa* was born.

Many glorious and strong winyanboga have inspired and supported this work in large and small ways by workshopping or performing in the play and encouraging me.

Thank you to Deidre Bux, Vicki Couzens, Felicia Dean, Caroline Martin, Greta Morgan, Hilda Stewart, Lyn Thorpe, Zeta Thomson, Laurel Robinson, Alana Valentine, Ursula Yovich, Christine Anu, Miranda Tapsell, Elaine Crombie, Angeline Penrith, Nakkiah Lui, Susie Dee, Patricia Cornelius, Kylie Farmer, Tessa Rose, Leah Purcell, Nicole Foreshew, Lynette Narkle, Irma Woods, Rae Hodgson, Matilda Brown, Kylie Coolwell, Alexis Lane, Pamela Young, Danièle Hromek, Karen Norris, Nadeena Dixon, Alison Murphy-Oates, Liza-Mare Syron, Lily Shearer, Lou Bennett and my beautiful niece Dayna James-French.

These are but a few winyanboga who are shining brighter than the sun, fighting against incredible odds to nurture and represent family, community, culture and country. I thank you for your generosity and spirit in the creation of this play which has most definitely been guided by the indomitable spirit of my Granny Kitty, Auntie Hyllus Maris and her good friend and colleague Sonia Borg who remain champions for one of the most poetic, true and strong representations of Aboriginal Women today.

Andrea James

Winyanboga Yurringa was developed with support from Playwriting Australia and was first produced by Moogahlin Performing Arts at Carriageworks, Sydney, on 3 August 2016 with the following cast:

JADAH	Matilda Brown
MARGIE	Kylie Coolwell
CHANTELLE	Alexis Lane
WANDA	Angeline Penrith
NEECY	Tessa Rose
CAROL	Pamela Young

Director, Andrea James
Assistant Director, Dr Liza-Mare Syron
Dramaturg, Patricia Cornelius
Set and Costume Design, Danièle Hromek
Sound and A/V Design, Phil Downing
Lighting Design, Karen Norris
A/V Artist, Bindi Cole
Object Design and Weaving Consultant, Nadeena Dixon
Cultural Object Design, Steven Russell and Auntie Phyllis Stewart
Stage Manager, Grace Benn
Production Manager, Aiden Brennan

CHARACTERS

NEECY, a woman in her 50s, community leader

JADAH, a young urban woman in her 30s, a photographer at the edge of a stellar career, a fair-skinned Aboriginal woman

CHANTELLE, Neecy's 15-year-old niece, sharp, troubled, at risk, yet full of creative potential

WANDA, Neecy's cousin, 42 years old, a woman from the mission in town, has five children and maybe one on the way

MARGIE, Wanda's younger sister, just turned 40, works as a park ranger on her own country

CAROL, Neecy's cousin from the city, manager of an Indigenous Unit at a large-scale major museum, always impeccably dressed and self-styled, well-read, self-protective and earnest, remains serially single despite great effort to attract a mate

SETTING

Winyanboga Yurringa is set on a sandy and well-loved campsite on the banks of a wide, brown and swift-flowing inland river. River red gums surround the camp as far as the eye can see. Somewhere there is a horizon. There is a fireplace at the centre of the stage. Fires have been lit here for centuries.

PROLOGUE: WINYANBOGA YURRINGA

The land stretches out before us like a blank canvas. There is a sense of timelessness.

NEECY *has come from a great distance.*

She listens to country. She is seeking permission. She looks to a flock of birds that pass overhead. She listens some more. She feels. She waits. She calls out to the old ones.

NEECY: *Dhama Yenbena* [Old People].
    Dhama Winya [Old Woman].
    Dhama Yiyirr [Old Man].
    Dhama Mulana [Old Spirit].

    Permission is granted.

    She pulls a digging stick from her bag.

Boondi [A girl's best friend].
Nanyirr [Stick].
Winyarrin nanyirr [Women's digging stick].

    She begins to dig in the sand.

Bunburra djikurra. To Dig. Dig, dig. Get in there. Dig deep. Open up.

    Dive in. Opening up the eyes of the earth. Grub about. Get dirty. Get in. We dig. We reveal that which does not want to be seen. *Bunburra.*

    NEECY *digs a large hole in the sand. Lights reveal* NEECY's *niece,* CHANTELLE, *sitting off to the side with iPod and wearing headphones, sulking.*

CHANTELLE: Can we go now?

SCENE ONE

The sound of an approaching minibus and the twang of loud country 'n' western music. The bus screeches to a halt and the women alight from it noisily. Dust travels into the space, quickly followed by WANDA,

MARGIE *and* CAROL. *The language comes hard and fast and overlaps, disturbing the peace.*

WANDA: My moom is killing me?
CAROL: There musta been about …
MARGIE: We're here!
CAROL: … one thousand potholes …
MARGIE: At last!
CAROL: … in that road.
MARGIE: Not that many.
CAROL: There was!
MARGIE: The road's not that bad.
CAROL: I counted every one of them.
WANDA: We woulda got here sooner …
MARGIE: … if we didn't have to pick up Carol …
WANDA: … who was an hour late!
CAROL: I had a few things at work I had to finish off.
MARGIE: We waited for ages …
CAROL: Don't blame me for being late! We spent nearly two hours in the supermarket buying food.
WANDA: Tim Tams are very important!
CAROL: Why did we have to have a conference in aisle three about what brand of baked beans we should get …?
WANDA: I like yellow and gold!
MARGIE: I told you! It's Heinz or nothing.
WANDA: Yellow and gold! You save at least fifty cents!
MARGIE: They don't say 'Heinz Meanz Beanzzzz' for nothing!
WANDA: It's 'Beanz Meanz Heinz'.
MARGIE: Whatever.
CAROL: Then we waited for an hour at the butchers!
MARGIE: Why didn't we get meat at the supermarket?
WANDA: I like to support the local butcher.
CAROL: That guy behind the counter was hot.
MARGIE: He was disgusting!
CAROL: He was lovely.
MARGIE: He had a goatee!
CAROL: Did not!

WANDA: I told you he was good-looking, didn't I, Carol?

MARGIE: You should've asked him out.

WANDA: I've already got a man.

MARGIE: Not you! Carol shoulda asked him for a date.

CAROL: No way! He's good-looking, but I'm not that desperate!

WANDA: What about you, Margie, he's a single man with a good job in town.

MARGIE: Don't be stupid, Wanda, he looked like Catweazle. He's not my type.

WANDA: Mmm, he does have good biceps.

MARGIE: Must be from lifting all of those carcasses.

CAROL: Wanda ordered a side of lamb.

MARGIE: He cut it up then and there.

WANDA: I like my meat fresh.

CAROL: Then we had to wait around forever while Margie put all her camping gear in the bus.

MARGIE: A girl can never be too prepared.

WANDA: What do we need a GPS tracking device for?!

MARGIE: To record our co-ordinates!

WANDA: I don't think we've been very 'co-ordinated' thus far.

CAROL: I'll tell you what made me unco-ordinated. Wanda's music!

CAROL and MARGIE: [*together*] / A wanga nang, a wanga nang, a wanga nang …

WANDA: /What's wrong with Johnny Cash?!

CAROL: Not on high rotation!

CAROL and MARGIE: [*together*] / A wanga nang, a wanga nang, a wanga nang …

CAROL: /She played that same song over and over and over. My ears are still ringing!

MARGIE: And then Carol spewed!

CAROL: I told you I get carsick!

NEECY: [*shouting*] For goodness sake! You're here now. Breathe in that fresh air.

> *They all breathe in and take in the fresh air.*
>
> *Pause.*
>
> *The women notice* CHANTELLE, *sulking, with her headphones on.*

WANDA: Which way?

MARGIE: She alright?

NEECY: Mmm.

CAROL: I heard.

NEECY: Lucky she didn't get killed.

CAROL: Stolen?

NEECY: Full cop chase, the works …

MARGIE: Who was driving?

NEECY: Who do you think?

MARGIE: Dickhead.

NEECY: She'll have to go to court. [*Whispering*] And she's skipped a period.

MARGIE and CAROL: [*together*] What?!

NEECY: Took the contraceptive patch off her arm.

> CHANTELLE *has been listening all along. She takes her headset off.*

CHANTELLE: That patch made me look like a slut!

CAROL: Chantelle! Nice to see you too!

WANDA: Hello, darlin'.

MARGIE: Love you too …

CAROL: You alright?

CHANTELLE: Yes!

MARGIE: You sure?

CHANTELLE: I'm fine!

> CAROL, WANDA *and* MARGIE *give* CHANTELLE *a playful kiss.* CHANTELLE *resists.*

NEECY: Well, we're here now!

> *Pause.*

WANDA: Now what?

NEECY: We gotta say hello to country.

> *There's an awkward silence. Each woman searching for a way to say hello to country. Not sure what to do.*

Let them spirits know we're back home.

> *More silence.* CHANTELLE *checks for mobile phone reception.*

Let them know we're here.

Pause.

We're home.

Pause.

CAROL: I still feel carsick …

SCENE TWO

The women enter and exit carrying loads of swags, eskys, camping furniture and equipment from the bus. Their huge pile of gear forms a mound on the land. CHANTELLE *is seated, gloomily listening to music through her headphones.* CAROL *struggles with a fold-out camping chair.* MARGIE *enters with a camping oven.*

MARGIE: Okay, ladies, never fear, 'cause Ranger Margie is here with the best little camping oven this side of the Southern Hemisphere. I inherited this little cast iron beauty from Nana Alice. I reckon them old ladies have cooked about a thousand stews in this little baby.

She exits to get more gear.

CAROL: Now this here is my favourite bit of camping equipment. Check this out!

She unfolds the chair, sits in it, puts her feet up on a fold-out camping stool, pulls out a plastic champagne flute from her handbag, puts it in the cup holder in the arm of the camping chair and clicks her fingers.

Waiter!

WANDA: Did you really bring champagne?!

CAROL: Of course! It's in the esky.

NEECY enters with the esky and exits to get more gear.

I brought some Bombay Sapphire too. Nothing like a gin and tonic to watch the sun go down.

WANDA prepares drinks, MARGIE *enters struggling with a table.*

MARGIE: Here, Chantelle, help me set up this table.

CHANTELLE is still sitting listening to music. MARGIE *pulls one of the headphones from her ear.*

I said help me set up this table.

CHANTELLE: There's no mobile phone reception!

MARGIE: Now!

> CHANTELLE *reluctantly helps* MARGIE.

[*Indicating to* CAROL *and* WANDA] Good to see ya two aunties here giving us a hand!

CAROL: You wanna G&T, Margie? Let's have a wind-down. We've been working our mooms off all week!

CHANTELLE: Can I have some too?

WANDA, CAROL and MARGIE: [*together*] No!

WANDA: You're too young.

CHANTELLE: I've drunk gin before.

WANDA: Who gave you that?

CHANTELLE: All my friends drink.

CAROL: It's no good for developing brains.

MARGIE: I saw that on the '7.30 Report'.

CHANTELLE: What about your brain?

CAROL: I'm an adult.

MARGIE: Come on, Chantelle, let's set up camp before it gets dark.

CHANTELLE: This is slave labour!

MARGIE: Where can I set up our clothesline?

WANDA: Bloody hell, Margie! I've come here to get away from the housework!

MARGIE: A girl can never be too prepared. Where are those pegs?

CHANTELLE: How would I know?!

> MARGIE *exits.*

WANDA: I've got enough dirty washing waiting for me at home.

CAROL: I've got a PhD deadline waiting for me at home.

CHANTELLE: I've got my boyfriend waiting for me at home.

CAROL: I've got nobody waiting for me at home.

> MARGIE *enters with more gear.*

MARGIE: I've got my … dog waiting for me at home.

WANDA: Shoulda asked that butcher out!

MARGIE: That's Carol's boyfriend, not mine!

CHANTELLE: Catweazle?!

WANDA: He was lovely.

MARGIE: He'd be making good money.

WANDA: He had soft hands.

CHANTELLE: You looked at his hands?!

MARGIE: Can't go wrong with a small business man, Carol.

> MARGIE *exits.*

WANDA: Yeah, Carol, he'd be making heaps of dough. And you'd get free meat.

CAROL: Enough with the butcher!

> MARGIE *re-enters with a camping shower.*

MARGIE: This camping shower warms up the water in the sun. I'll string it up on this tree over here.

CAROL: Thank God you brought a shower!

CHANTELLE: I need to wash my hair in the morning.

WANDA: Bloody hell, Margie! You sure you didn't pack the kitchen sink?!

> MARGIE *re-enters with a kitchen sink.*

MARGIE: What ya say, Wanda?

> *The ladies laugh.*

CAROL: Well, ladies, here's to being back at home.

> *They clink their tin cups.*

WANDA and CAROL: [*together*] To home!

> NEECY *enters and spots the women drinking.*

NEECY: Pour it out.

CAROL: Come on, Neecy!

NEECY: I said pour it out.

WANDA: Don't be a spoil sport!

NEECY: Carol …

CAROL: We're just having a sundowner.

NEECY: I said pour it out.

> *The women look to each other and pour their drinks in the sand.* NEECY *grabs the bottle.*

SCENE THREE

MARGIE *is setting up some camping equipment.* CHANTELLE *approaches her.*

CHANTELLE: Auntie Margie, you know this country pretty well, ay?

MARGIE: Like the back of my hand.

CHANTELLE: How far is the nearest town from here?

MARGIE: Oooh, it's a long ways off.

CHANTELLE: How far?

MARGIE: Would take you about three hours to walk out of here.

CHANTELLE: Three hours to walk to the nearest town! Do you get mobile reception there?

MARGIE: It's a bit weak, gotta go up on the big hill at the park. There's a phone box at the post office though.

CHANTELLE: Which way?

MARGIE: Well, If you go that way you gotta take a turn left about ten k's down, then right at the fork, then right, then right again—but you can't always go that way, because the river's in flood that way. It's over the road. I wouldn't cross the river. You'd drown. So you gotta do a big loop. Or, you can go up over the big sandhill past the big bend, but you gotta go through this farmer's property and he's got dogs. I wouldn't go that way. Or, you can go right around the swamp over at rat's castle, you take a right and then two lefts …

CHANTELLE: Which way?

MARGIE: … but you gotta watch for the king brown snakes.

CHANTELLE: King browns?!

MARGIE: They're nesting at the moment and they'll chase ya. Best to go by car if you go that way. But you gotta make sure you don't get bogged.

CHANTELLE: Bogged?! I'm stuck in this hell hole!

MARGIE: Yes! And your Auntie Margie is the Devil! Come here, my sweet! Ahahahahaha!

> MARGIE *plays with kidnapping* CHANTELLE.

CHANTELLE: Auntie Marg? Reckon I can borrow twenty dollars?

MARGIE: What for?

CHANTELLE: Pleeeease?

> *Pause.*

MARGIE: Alright then! But don't tell ya aunt!

> MARGIE *gives* CHANTELLE *twenty bucks.*

> NEECY *and* CAROL *enter with a big cardboard box and place it in the space.*

CHANTELLE: What's in there?!

NEECY: None of your business. Okay, ladies, better set up our beds before it gets dark.

CAROL: Are we sleeping outside?

NEECY: What did you think we were gonna do?

CAROL: There's dirt everywhere.

MARGIE: We're in the bush! We're camping.

CAROL: I've brought my new pillows. They're gonna get ruined.

The women start to set up their swags.

MARGIE: What ya need, Carol, is a good dry-as-a-bone swag.

CAROL: What I need, is a campervan with all the mod cons.

MARGIE *rolls out her swag.*

WANDA: Not there, that's my spot!

MARGIE: Wanda! Why do you have to sleep in the same spot every time?!

WANDA: Because this is my spot! It's always been my spot! And that's Mum's spot and that's Dad's spot.

NEECY: You two have been arguing about this since you were five.

MARGIE: You always choose the spot that's closest to the fire.

WANDA: I like my head to go that way. Besides, you've got ya 'dry-as-a-bone' swag. Put it to some use!

MARGIE: Yeah, and then if we get attacked by an axe murderer at night, I'll be the one he gets first.

CAROL: Axe murderer?!

CHANTELLE: Can we go home now?!

NEECY: There's no axe murderer!

WANDA: Or a prison escapee!

CAROL: Shut up!

WANDA: With an axe!

NEECY: There are no prison escapees either.

WANDA: What about Dhurringile Prison Farm? If a fulla wanted to get out and not be found, this is where he'd come.

CHANTELLE: Or some creepy guy called Mick will offer us a lift into town in his HQ Statesman.

NEECY: That is a movie, Chantelle. This is real life.

CHANTELLE: We're going to die!

CAROL: I've gotta have a coony.

NEECY: Thanks for sharing.

CAROL: Where am I gonna go?!

NEECY: Out there!

MARGIE *grabs her shovel and toilet paper.*

MARGIE: Lucky I packed these.

CAROL: No thanks. I'll wait.

WANDA: You'll get backed up if you don't go now.

CAROL: I'll wait till I get back home.

WANDA: Bloody hell!

CAROL: My pillow's got dirt on it already.

CHANTELLE: Gee, Aunt, you sure you couldn't find a frillier pillow?

CAROL: This is my favourite pillow. I brought two. [*Searching for her other pillow*] I can't sleep without two pillows.

CHANTELLE: What are we gonna do if it rains?

CAROL: Rain?!

NEECY: It won't rain.

MARGIE: And if it does, you just put up the flap of your swag. See here.

She demonstrates.

WANDA: And keep watch for the axe murderer.

MARGIE: Shut up! Fire hog!

CHANTELLE: How long are we staying here for?

NEECY: As long as it takes.

CHANTELLE: What?!

CAROL: Just like the old days.

MARGIE: Camping in the bush with my sisters.

WANDA: And an axe murderer.

MARGIE, CHANTELLE, CAROL and NEECY: [*together*] Shut up!

A car arrives.

WANDA: Who's this, turning up so late?

MARGIE: It's getting dark.

WANDA: Are we expecting someone?

CHANTELLE: What sort of car is it?

CAROL: I'm not sure.

WANDA: Sounds like a V8.

MARGIE: Bogans.

CHANTELLE: Is it a HQ Statesman?
WANDA: Can't tell.
CHANTELLE: Sounds like a HQ Statesman.
MARGIE: I'll get my gun!
NEECY: You packed your gun?!
MARGIE: I'm always on bogan patrol.
NEECY: Do not get that gun out of the van.
CHANTELLE: It's The Axe Murderer!
WANDA: Mick! The Axe Murderer!

They huddle.

SCENE FOUR

A figure enters and stands in silhouette. The women are terrified. NEECY
recognises JADAH.

JADAH: Hello?
NEECY: Jadah? Great to see you.

They hug.

Find your way here alright?
JADAH: Sorry about the noise. Ripped my muffler off doing a U-turn in
the bush. I went the wrong way, but I backtracked my way here.
NEECY: Everyone. This is Jadah.
WANDA: [*to* MARGIE] What did she bring a white woman here for?
MARGIE: Dunno.
NEECY: Jadah's our photographer.
WANDA: What do we need a photographer for?
CAROL: This is an historical moment.
NEECY: That's right.

Pause.

WANDA: Where ya from?
JADAH: Ah … Melbourne. At the moment. I travel around a bit.
NEECY: This is our great-great-grandmother's dreaming place.
JADAH: It's beautiful.
NEECY: This is my niece Chantelle, my cousin Margie—sister to Wanda
here—and you already know Carol.
JADAH: Hi, Carol.

NEECY: It's good to finally be back here on country.

Here with my sisters.

Silence.

SCENE FIVE

JADAH *stands awkwardly holding her swag and bedding. She is unsure where to camp and attempts to lay out her swag.*

WANDA: Not there!

MARGIE: That's Wanda's spot.

CHANTELLE: Yeah, I wouldn't sleep next to Auntie Wanda.

MARGIE: She snores!

WANDA: [*sarcastically*] Ha ha!

JADAH *goes to set up her swag next to* MARGIE.

Not there!

CHANTELLE: I wouldn't get too close to Auntie Margie either!

WANDA: Yeah, 'specially after she's eaten those 'Heinz Meanz Beanzzz'.

MARGIE: You mean 'Beanz Meanz Heinz'.

WANDA: / Whatever!

CHANTELLE *makes a farting noise ...*

MARGIE: Ha ha! Very funny.

JADAH *doesn't know where to put her swag down.*

NEECY: Come over here, Jadah, and set up next to me and Chantelle.

CHANTELLE *sees* JADAH's *new bag.*

CHANTELLE: Flash bag you got there!

JADAH: Thanks.

MARGIE: Where'd you get that from?

JADAH: New York.

MARGIE *and* WANDA *look at each other.*

WANDA and MARGIE: [*together*] Ooh la la.

MARGIE: New York!

CHANTELLE: Mad!

JADAH: I had a residency there last year.

MARGIE: You've got a *house* in New York!

CAROL: An 'artist's residency', Margie.

NEECY: Jadah had a studio in New York last year.

JADAH: In Chelsea. They gave me a one-year scholarship.

WANDA: I hope we're not too 'downtown' for you here.

NEECY: She's back home now, aren't you, Jadah?

> CHANTELLE *grabs* JADAH*'s bag and starts to prance about with it, singing a homespun rap song about New York.*

CHANTELLE: Did ya get to see Jayzee?

JADAH: Nah, Jayzee lives in LA.

CHANTELLE: What was New York like?

JADAH: Amazing. Freaks and artists and beggars and rich people everywhere.

CHANTELLE: Did you climb the Statue of Liberty?

JADAH: Yep.

CHANTELLE: Travel the subway?

JADAH: Every day.

CHANTELLE: Did ya get mugged?

JADAH: Only once.

CHANTELLE: Did ya see Spiderman?

JADAH: I wish …

CHANTELLE: Did you eat buffalo burgers?

JADAH: Yep. With fries!

CHANTELLE: I'm starving! Is there food in that box?

> CHANTELLE *goes to open the big cardboard box.*

CAROL: Don't touch that!

CHANTELLE: Why?!

NEECY: Just leave it there.

> NEECY *and* CAROL *sit down next to the box as if they're guarding it.*

Now, women, this here is a very historical moment …

CHANTELLE: Do we have access to power?

WANDA: There's no electricity.

CHANTELLE: What?! No electricity?! No wi-fi! How am I gonna Facebook?

NEECY: Enough. Now …

CHANTELLE: I'm starving! When are we gonna eat?

NEECY: Now, women …

CAROL: Spider! There's a spider on me!

MARGIE: Where?!

CAROL: Get it off me! Get it off me!

MARGIE: There's no spider!

CAROL: It's in my hair! I can feel it crawling— /

WANDA: / There's nothing there— /

CAROL: / Get it off me get it off me get it off me.

WANDA: There's nothing there.

MARGIE: Calm down.

CAROL: I hate spiders!

NEECY: Shoosh!

CAROL: She said shoosh!

> *Pause.*

NEECY: At last. Peace. Quiet. Country. Watch with your eyes! Listen with your heart! We've been coming to this spot for hundreds and hundreds of years. For as long as I can remember and as long as my mother can remember, and her mother too. I've brought you all here …

> CHANTELLE *gets up to open a packet of Tim Tams.*

I've brought you all here …

WANDA: I could really do with a cup of tea.

NEECY: … so that we can …

MARGIE: I'll go get my billy!

> MARGIE *runs to the car.*

NEECY: I give up! Chantelle, come with me, we're gonna need some more firewood! I can see this is gonna be a very long night.

CHANTELLE: Do I have to?

NEECY: Yes!

CHANTELLE: Getting firewood is men's business!

NEECY: Since when?!

WANDA and CAROL: [*together*] You wanna watch out for that hairy bekka!

CHANTELLE: What's a hairy bekka?

NEECY: Now, you ladies, make sure Jadah feels at home.

> NEECY *exits, followed quickly by* CHANTELLE.

SCENE SIX

CAROL *and* WANDA *are drinking cups of tea and eating Tim Tams.* WANDA *watches* JADAH *as she takes photos of the trees, river and surrounds.* MARGIE *enters with a huge Hong Kong bag.*

MARGIE: Here we go!

> *She plonks down the bag.*

Grass!

WANDA: Grass! I thought you gave up smoking.

MARGIE: Weaving grass, Wanda. I've been drying this up for weeks.

> MARGIE *hands bunches of grass to the women who start to pre- pare it for weaving.*

JADAH: Basket weaving! My grandmother had one of those on her man- telpiece. Mind if I take a few photos?

> *The women look at each other.*

MARGIE: S'pose.

WANDA: Just don't take any photos of me!

MARGIE: You love having your photo taken.

WANDA: Not by complete strangers.

CAROL: Take as many of me as you like. I'm very photogenic.

> JADAH *takes a few snaps as* MARGIE *and* CAROL *pose ironically.*

MARGIE: You can put our photos in your next exhibition!

WANDA: You could call it [*dramatically*] 'Real Housewives of Cummeragunja'.

CAROL: I hope you got my right angle!

WANDA: Just don't take any photos of me. Ya got that?

JADAH: Yep. Got it.

> CAROL *grabs the weaving from the Hong Kong bag.*

CAROL: Margie. Give me a hand with this stitch. I always have trouble remembering how to start.

MARGIE: This here's ya point and this is ya tail. You loop this around here twice and then away you go.

CAROL: You always make it look so easy.

MARGIE *and* CAROL *weave together in time. Like a dance.*

MARGIE: Why'd you come out here, Carol, you hate camping.

CAROL: To get away from that bloody office of mine!

WANDA: Those fellas still giving you a hard time?

CAROL: Museum testosterone. I think it's shrinking my brain …

MARGIE: You making alright money though?

CAROL: Yeah, but I've got no life! You've gotta work twice as hard to prove yourself to the suits upstairs.

MARGIE: Bloody men.

WANDA: What's wrong with men?!

CAROL: At the end of the day I'm just coming home to a cold, dark kitchen.

WANDA: You just need a good man.

MARGIE: You'd know all about that, wouldn't you, Wanda!?

CAROL: Don't talk to me about men. I'm surprised that no-one in the office can hear my clock ticking.

'Carol, what's that booming sound I can hear? Oh, that's nothing, Madeline, it's just the sound of another fertile egg crashing into the oblivion.'

You've gotta put on a good show for the team, let them know they have a fearless leader.

MARGIE: That's why you've gotta stick with it, sis.

CAROL: I think I've blown it this time.

MARGIE: What do you mean?

CAROL: Never mind.

MARGIE: Don't let them drag you down.

CAROL: Remember when Nana Therese taught us to weave?

MARGIE: She was a tough old bird alright.

CAROL: Yeah, she used to say, 'You gotta split the grass like this. Exactly the same every time.'

They split grass beautifully in time. JADAH *takes a series of close-ups of the women's hands and weaving.*

'This little fella. That's what will make your basket neat. No no, not like that! Like this! You gotta *relax* into the weaving. If you're thinking grumpy, you'll make a messy basket.'

MARGIE: [*whispering*] And every now and then she'd look over her shoulder. To make sure no-one was looking.

CAROL: [*whispering*] Grandma Cilla was too scared that her daughter would be taken away if the missionaries caught her weaving.

MARGIE: [*whispering*] They wouldn't let the old people speak any of their language or sing any of their songs.

CAROL: [*whispering*] Nana Therese used to weave late at night in her room. In the dark with bits of ribbon, bits of raffia.

MARGIE: [*whispering*] Whatever she could get her hands on.

CAROL: [*whispering*] Why are we whispering?

They laugh.

MARGIE: Just habit I guess.

CAROL: Some of Nan's baskets are in the museum.

MARGIE: True.

CAROL: With her signature stitch.

MARGIE: That red grass she used to find.

CAROL: When I'm having a bad day, I'll go down to the archives and sit with Nan's baskets.

MARGIE: That red grass! I've looked for it everywhere.

CAROL: It'll turn up.

Silence. The women weave.

MARGIE: If it wasn't for Nana Therese, we woulda lost this weaving forever.

CAROL: Nana Therese was weaving in the dark, for us, so that now we can weave in the light.

JADAH *takes photos.*

CAROL *checks to see if* WANDA *is in earshot.*

Have you told Wanda yet?

MARGIE: God, no! I haven't been to her house since that dickhead moved in.

CAROL: She'll come round, sis.

CAROL *exits only to return quickly and furtively to take her shoulder bag.*

MARGIE: Jadah! Here you go. Come and split this grass.

JADAH *sits with them.*

Just get your fingernail in the centre and strip it like this!

MARGIE *demonstrates.* JADAH *splits the grass awkwardly and cuts herself.*

JADAH: Ouch! Shit!

WANDA: Looks like Madam New York has cut herself!

MARGIE: Lucky I brought my first-aid kit!

WANDA: Of course you did!

MARGIE: A girl can never be too prepared.

She passes a bandaid to JADAH.

Hurts like hell, ay?

JADAH: Sure does.

MARGIE: You gotta say 'hello' to the grass before you work it. That's the one.

JADAH *strips the grass a few times. She starts to get the hang of it.*

You've driven a long way here?

JADAH: All the way from Brunswick.

MARGIE: That's a long way, isn't it?

JADAH: Yeah, it's a long way.

MARGIE: You come out bush often?

JADAH: Nah, not really.

MARGIE: You don't come out bush often?

JADAH: No.

MARGIE: But you like the bush?

JADAH: Yeah. Love it.

MARGIE: But you don't come out that much?

JADAH: No.

MARGIE: And you take photographs?

JADAH: Yeah.

MARGIE: And you're an artist?

JADAH: Yep.

MARGIE: And Neecy wants you to take photos?

JADAH: Yep.

MARGIE: What kind of photos?

JADAH: Documentation.

MARGIE: Documentation?

JADAH: For Neecy.

MARGIE: For Neecy?

MARGIE: But you're not from the bush.

JADAH: Melbourne born and bred.

MARGIE: Melbourne born and bred.

WANDA: Bloody hell, Margie! What are you a bloody detective?

MARGIE: Just catching up. [*To* JADAH] There ya go, you're getting the hang of that grass stripping! You've got this whole bunch to do now.

> *She hands her a big bunch of grass.* WANDA *and* MARGIE *exit.*

SCENE SEVEN

CAROL is out bush sitting on a tree stump. She holds a glass of wine. She sips and watches the sunset. NEECY *and* CHANTELLE *enter with firewood in their arms.*

CAROL: Neecy!

> *She does a little dance with her wine glass trying to hide it from* NEECY.

You frightened me. I just went away from camp for some quiet time.

NEECY: What are you doing, Carol?

CAROL: Nothing!

CHANTELLE: What's up, Auntie Carol?

NEECY: Chantelle, go and get some more kindling.

CHANTELLE: What?!

NEECY: Before it gets dark. Over there.

CHANTELLE: I'm not going out there on my own!

NEECY: We can see you. Go on.

> CHANTELLE *stands her ground.*

Go on. Go!

> CHANTELLE *reluctantly leaves.*

I thought I told you ladies, no drinking while we're on country.

CAROL: I'm just having a quiet red. This is a good pinot.

NEECY: No grog while we're on country.

CAROL: Come on, Neecy, give me a break!

NEECY: You know the deal.

CAROL: I just need it to relax. I get fidgety. Can't wind down. Can't stop thinking about work. They're always watching.

NEECY: You're not at work now, you're here.

CAROL: I'm always at work!

NEECY: Come on.

CAROL: I could lose my job over this!

NEECY: That's no excuse.

CAROL: How am I gonna pay my mortgage? I'll lose my apartment.

NEECY: You can come and stay at our place. We won't let them throw you out on the street.

CAROL: Uncle Albert hasn't spoken to me since I took on this job.

NEECY: He'll come round.

CAROL: I can handle it when the whitefellas run me down, but not when my own mob do.

NEECY: We need you in that museum.

CAROL: I've put my job on the line for you!

CHANTELLE *enters with a few twigs.*

CHANTELLE: There ya go, I got more sticks.

NEECY: That's not enough.

CHANTELLE: What?!

NEECY: Go get some more.

CHANTELLE *exits again.*

CAROL: I could go to gaol!

NEECY: You'll be right, Carol.

CAROL: Then I'll be no use to anyone.

NEECY: Hang in there, darling.

CAROL: That CEO is watching me like a hawk!

NEECY: That's because he's scared you're gonna take his job.

CAROL: The only black woman in senior management and they treat me like I'm a mad woman whenever I talk about cultural protocols.

NEECY: That's 'cause you've got a responsibility to your people.

CAROL: I had the elders bashing down my door when they took those bark paintings back to the London Museum.

NEECY: It was a court order!

CAROL: Try telling that to the mob. Those bark paintings are painted with our blood. Auntie Faye cried for weeks about those barks.

NEECY: You did the best you could.

CAROL: I couldn't keep those barks in the country.

NEECY: That was the whitefulla law did that, not ours.

CAROL: Broke my heart, Neecy.

NEECY: We're on country now. We've got important business to do.

CAROL: I don't know if these women are up to it.

NEECY: They better be, I told Bob I'd be back in two days.

CAROL: How is Bob?

NEECY: At home feeding the dogs and keeping an eye on the garden.

CAROL: You've got yourself a good man there.

NEECY: He puts up with my crazy family!

CAROL: Are you sure we're not gonna get Jadah into trouble?

NEECY: She'll be right. Come on, let's settle in for the night and we'll do it tomorrow.

CAROL: I'll just finish this glass and I'll meet you back later.

NEECY: Uh-uh. Come on.

CAROL: I won't be able to get to sleep.

NEECY: We've got business to do.

CAROL: Watch my back, Neecy.

NEECY: I'm watching it.

> CAROL *sneaks one last swig of her glass.*

SCENE EIGHT

Back at the camp MARGIE *and* WANDA *are preparing a stew.* JADAH *is stripping the grass.*

WANDA: Why don't you stop over for the night on the way back home?

MARGIE: Can't. I've gotta get back home and feed the animals.

WANDA: The kids miss you, they're always asking, 'Where's Auntie?'

MARGIE: Auntie's busy.

WANDA: It's been a long time since you visited.

MARGIE: I work late at night.

WANDA: I don't like you driving back home in the dark on those roads.

MARGIE: I'm alright, sis, you know I love my job.

WANDA: We only live in the town next door, you know!

MARGIE: I know!

> *Silence. They chop onions.*

WANDA: You've gotta go out more.

MARGIE: You've seen where I live. Where do you go out?!

WANDA: Go to the pub! There's lots of eligible young bachelors at the pub.

MARGIE: Pfffft! As if!

WANDA: Or the footy club. Lots of good-looking blackfellas at the footy club.

MARGIE: Wanda, I'm alright.

WANDA: Or take up a hobby. That's a good way to meet new people.

MARGIE: I've got my weaving.

WANDA: You're not gonna meet a bloke sitting around weaving. Join a sport team—mixed soccer or something.

MARGIE: Wanda, I can't stand soccer!

WANDA: Where are you gonna meet blokes?

MARGIE: I'm not interested in meeting blokes!

WANDA: I have no trouble meeting blokes and I live in a smaller town than you do.

Silence. They chop onions.

MARGIE: That man of yours still staying at your house?

WANDA: None of your business.

MARGIE: Do the kids like him?

WANDA: Little Taryn follows him around the house all day like a little chick.

MARGIE: So he's still not working then?

WANDA: What's it to you?

MARGIE: Always seems to have enough money to get out of it!

WANDA: What would you know?

MARGIE: He's gonna muck up your pension hanging around your house like a bad smell.

WANDA: He helps out!

MARGIE: You don't need a handyman, sis!

WANDA: I do!

MARGIE: You need a fulla who can provide.

WANDA: I'm doing alright!

MARGIE: Wanda, it's not alright. You're my sister, and you deserve better than this.

WANDA: Pass me the bloody capsicum!

MARGIE *passes the capsicum to* WANDA *and they chop veggies.*

MARGIE: You right there, sis?

WANDA: Yeah …

MARGIE: You okay?

WANDA: Yeah. It's the bloody onions. Shit!

SCENE NINE

CHANTELLE *and* CAROL *enter carrying armloads of wood.* NEECY *follows, dragging a big log.*

NEECY: Here ya go … this'll keep us going all night.

MARGIE: Good one, Neece.

NEECY: No thanks to this one here who jumped every time she heard a twig snap.

CHANTELLE: I did not!

NEECY: Come here, my little Chantelle bell. You've been a good hunter gatherer. And now we're gonna keep warm for the night, see?

She wraps her arm around CHANTELLE *for a photo.*

Jadah, take a photo of me and my *lovely* niece.

JADAH *takes a snap and is interrupted by her mobile phone ringing.*

JADAH: Sorry, Neecy, just gotta take this call.

CHANTELLE: Her phone is working? Why is her phone working? Mine's dead!

WANDA: She's got a yuppie phone.

MARGIE: She's got an iPhone.

WANDA: Yup—iPhone.

CAROL: My phone doesn't get any reception here either.

CHANTELLE: Why didn't she tell me her phone was working?!

CAROL: Or my iPad.

MARGIE: There's no wi-fi out here!

NEECY: We don't need phones or iPads or wi-fi here anyway.

CAROL: I was gonna do a bit of work on my thesis!

CHANTELLE: Auntie Neece, can I use Jadah's phone when she's finished?

NEECY: I told you to stay away from that fulla!

CHANTELLE: Who says I was gonna ring him?

NEECY: You know what? No phone calls or going out until after the court case. I'm taking your phone.

NEECY confiscates the phone from CHANTELLE.

CHANTELLE: This is a joke!

The women come in hard and fast.

CAROL: He's too old for you, Chantelle.

MARGIE: I don't like that car he drives.

CAROL: Or the dickheads he hangs around with.

MARGIE: And what's with that awful tattoo on his neck?

CHANTELLE: That's my name!

CAROL: Makes him look like a criminal.

MARGIE: Your name is on his neck for the rest of his life.

NEECY: Don't you go getting any tattoos on your neck. For Christ's sake!

MARGIE: And tell him to pull up his bloody pants.

NEECY: Why they gotta wear their pants like that?

MARGIE: With the jocks hanging out up the top.

NEECY: What's with that?

CHANTELLE: I just wanna ring him and let him know I got here okay.

CAROL: You've only been away for one day.

CHANTELLE: I told him I'd ring him as soon as we got here.

WANDA: Chill out! You were young once too. She's in love.

NEECY: 'In love', my moom.

CHANTELLE: I do love him!

NEECY: Oh yeah, is that why he ran off and left you in a smashed-up stolen car, stinking of dope?!

WANDA: Neecy, who made you Camp Leader? You haven't stopped telling us what to do since we got here.

CHANTELLE: I just wanna make a quick call.

NEECY: When you start going back to school, then you can have your phone privileges back.

CHANTELLE: Bullshit!

CAROL: Don't you talk to your auntie like that!

NEECY: I said no!

JADAH walks back into camp finishing her phone call.

WANDA: I remember my first boyfriend.

MARGIE: Andrew?!

WANDA: And my first kiss. It was like heaven. Down at the park on the swings with a full moon shining.

MARGIE: Shame he turned out to be such a dickhead.

NEECY: My first boyfriend was Colin.

MARGIE: I remember Colin! He was a cutie.

NEECY: He could do a triple somersault off the rope swing over the river and then do a horsie buck on entry into the water.

WANDA: Yeah, I bet that wasn't all he bucked!

CHANTELLE: Gross!

NEECY: Mum really loved Colin. He'd come over and eat us out of house and home. Real charmer he was. He had these shiny black ringlets and chocolate brown skin.

MARGIE: Where is he now?

NEECY: I dunno. He got married. Got fat. Had six hundred kids, living on his own in a flat.

WANDA: My first love. Andrew. He was real romantic.

MARGIE: He was a scruffy little twerp.

WANDA: He used to hold my hand when we were walking and we'd swim in the river together for hours and hours and hours.

MARGIE: And then you got pregnant.

WANDA: Well, yeah. Then I got pregnant.

MARGIE: And he took off. Real romantic like.

NEECY: What's he doing now?

WANDA: I dunno, got married, got fat, had six hundred kids, living on his own in a flat.

CAROL: My first fulla, he may as well have been a cardboard box.

MARGIE: Empty?

CAROL: Uh-uh!

WANDA: I remember that fulla. What was his name?

CAROL: Dean. He used to tense up like concrete every time I gave him a hug.

MARGIE: Real romantic.

WANDA: Cardboard man!

MARGIE: Some fella will come along soon.

CAROL: Every man in the city is either married up …

ALL: Or gay!

MARGIE: Or fat …

WANDA: With six hundred kids …

NEECY: Living on his own in a flat …

WANDA: Who was your first boyfriend, Margie?

MARGIE: Can't remember.

WANDA: Everyone remembers their first love.

MARGIE: It was a long time ago.

WANDA: You never forget your first love.

MARGIE: I can't remember.

WANDA: Oh well, he probably …

NEECY: Got fat …

CAROL: … had six hundred kids …

NEECY: … and is …

ALL: … living on his own in a flat …

CHANTELLE *quietly sidles up to* JADAH.

CHANTELLE: Jadah, can I check out your phone?

JADAH: Yeah, sure.

JADAH *keeps hold of her phone and* CHANTELLE *checks it out over her shoulder.*

CHANTELLE: iPhone X? Nice screen! Does this have facial recognition?

JADAH: Yep.

CHANTELLE: Unlimited data?

JADAH: Yep.

CHANTELLE *checks to see if* NEECY *is looking.*

CHANTELLE: [*whispering*] Can I use your phone to text my man?

JADAH: [*whispering*] I dunno, Chantelle.

CHANTELLE: [*whispering*] Please. Just one text.

JADAH: Ummmmmmmm?

CHANTELLE *looks over* JADAH*'s shoulder at her phone.*

CHANTELLE: Who's this on your phone?

JADAH: That's my cousin Leon.

CHANTELLE: He's lovely!

JADAH *swipes.*

JADAH: That's my Aunties Mavis and Heather. They live in Shepparton now. [*Swiping*] My cousins Jake … That's Alinta … Yolanda … [*Swiping*] This is me and my dad. Shady. He took me to the Poon's Chinese restaurant for my twenty-first.

CHANTELLE: Where's your mum?

JADAH: She died. When I was fourteen. Where's yours?

CHANTELLE: Gaol.

JADAH: Shit. What for?

CHANTELLE: Selling drugs for her boyfriend. Auntie Neecy's looking after me now.

Have you got a boyfriend?

JADAH: Kinda.

CHANTELLE: Reckon you'll have kids?

JADAH: I dunno. Maybe, when I've travelled a bit more. What about you?

CHANTELLE: Yeah. I want heaps. Biggest mobs. Chris reckons he's gonna get us a house.

JADAH: Yeah well, the party ends when you have kids.

CHANTELLE: [*looking back at* JADAH's *phone*] Who's that lady?

JADAH: That's my nan. Maryann Louise Melville.

> CHANTELLE *looks at the photo and then at* JADAH *and then back to the phone again.*

CHANTELLE: That's your nan?

JADAH: Yeah, she's beautiful, ay?

> CHANTELLE *looks at* JADAH *quizzically.* JADAH *hands her the phone …*

SCENE TEN

CHANTELLE *sits gloomily with her arms folded. The women are serving up dinner.*

NEECY: Come on, girls, dinner's ready.

> CHANTELLE *ignores her.*

Remember when we used to have those big cook-ups with Uncle Stubby? He'd come back from his hunting trip with a big kangaroo and an emu.

MARGIE: Every time!

NEECY: [*to* CHANTELLE] Get those bloody things out of your ear and join us for dinner.

CHANTELLE: I'm not eating kangaroo.

WANDA: And we used to laugh that hard, 'cause Mum used to joke that we were eating the national anthem!

CAROL: You mean the *national coat of arms*!

WANDA: Whatever!

NEECY: Chantelle, come and eat your dinner.

CHANTELLE: I'm not eating kangaroo.

> *The ladies start eating.*

MARGIE: It's beautiful.

WANDA: You should try emu.

NEECY: It used to take us *hours* to pluck that emu.

CAROL: Stinks like hell!

NEECY: You don't mind eating it though.

CAROL: And Uncle Max would come around with a big bag of yabbies.

NEECY: And Auntie Faye would make yabbie curry.

WANDA: With Keens!

NEECY: Come on, Chantelle!

MARGIE: And Uncle Stubby cooked that kangaroo under the ground and uncles and aunties and cousins would come around for miles.

WANDA: He was like the Pied Piper!

CAROL: Potatoes in their jackets.

WANDA: Corn.

MARGIE: Fish wrapped up in paperbark.

WANDA: Stop it now! My mouth's watering.

NEECY: After dinner we'd sit around that big fire with our big full bellies.

MARGIE: And tell stories.

CAROL: And sing and laugh.

NEECY: To all hours of the night.

> *The women look to sulky* CHANTELLE. *They sing the chorus of 'Pretty Woman'.*

CHANTELLE: Oh, God! Stop it!

> *The women keep singing.*

That is truly tragic!

The phone beeps in CHANTELLE*'s pocket.*

NEECY: What was that?

The phone beeps again.

  Chantelle?

CHANTELLE: What?

NEECY: Where is that mobile phone coming from?

CHANTELLE: What phone?

The phone beeps again.

JADAH: That's my phone. I lent it to Chantelle to …

She realises that NEECY *doesn't want* CHANTELLE *to call her boyfriend.*

CHANTELLE: Thanks a lot, Jadah!

NEECY: No mobile phone until you're back at school.

JADAH: I'm sorry, Neecy, I didn't realise.

CHANTELLE: It's Chris! He's texting me back!

NEECY: Over my dead body! Carol, get that phone off that girl.

CHANTELLE: [*to* NEECY] I wish you were dead!

CAROL: Have some respect!

NEECY: Wanda, get that phone off that girl! I'll throw the damn thing in the river!

WANDA *pulls the phone out of* CHANTELLE*'s hand.*

CHANTELLE: Give me the phone back! Bitch!

WANDA: What the—? What the fuck's this?

JADAH: It's from my gallery manager.

WANDA *passes the phone to* MARGIE.

MARGIE: Black Velvet? What the—?!

JADAH: It's the flier for my exhibition.

MARGIE *hands the phone to* NEECY.

NEECY: Jadah. What is this?

JADAH: It's a self-portrait!

WANDA: What the fuck?

JADAH: It's a still from an art performance.

WANDA: That's wrong …

She hands the phone to CAROL.

CAROL: Oh dear.

WANDA: She's got no clothes on!

JADAH: Can I have my phone back please?

WANDA *grabs the phone off* CAROL.

WANDA: What sort of sick, twisted portrait is this?!

NEECY: I don't understand.

JADAH: It's an artwork.

WANDA: It's porn!

NEECY: You shouldn't exhibit this.

MARGIE: That's not right.

WANDA: She's not right! What the fuck have you done to your pubes?!

JADAH: It's hair dye.

WANDA: That's our flag!

JADAH: I'm making a statement.

WANDA: About how gammin you are?

NEECY: Do your family know about this?

JADAH: Give me back my phone.

WANDA: Did you get funding from the government to do this?

JADAH: Can I have my phone back please?

WANDA: You need a slap across the face.

NEECY: Wanda! Stop it!

JADAH: I said, give me my phone!

JADAH *grabs her phone off* WANDA *and walks off.*

NEECY: Jadah, come back!

WANDA: You're a fake!

NEECY: Jadah!

WANDA: Nothing but a fake!

SCENE ELEVEN

JADAH *strips off her clothes to her singlet and undies and takes a long deep dive into the river. She floats and lets the current take her away.*

JADAH: Whiteness exposed
    My blackness flails about
    One punches the other

I am bruised
Inside and out
She's not my enemy
The enemy is within
Family trees
Branches lopped off
Blood spurts
This way and that
This is pure horror
I hate you
This black and this white
Within
This oil and this water
Cancelling me out
In equal measure
This is me
Claim me
Take me
Bleed me
This is me
I know this to be true
I am my father's daughter
From the freshwater
I am my grandmother's daughter
From the mountains, to the lakes, to the sea
I know this to be true
I am me
This here
This place here
Is me.

SCENE TWELVE

The women watch JADAH *from the riverbank.*

WANDA: I'm sick to death of white people coming into our communities
     and claiming to be one of us!
MARGIE: You can tell those mob a mile off.

WANDA: She's not even a half-caste!

CAROL: Wanda, we don't use words like that anymore.

WANDA: Smells like a Johnny-come-lately to me!

CAROL: Don't be ridiculous!

WANDA: They come in with a crazy fucked-up look in their eye. And they're always related to some princess!

MARGIE: And we don't even have princesses!

WANDA: Exactly! She looks white to me!

NEECY: Jesus, Wanda!

WANDA: She walks white, she talks white, she dresses white.

CAROL: Come on, Wanda, you don't even know the girl!

MARGIE: She *has* just rocked up out of the blue!

WANDA: How come we haven't seen her?

MARGIE: What's taken her so long?

CHANTELLE: I saw her nan's photo, Auntie, she's black as!

WANDA and MARGIE: [*together*] She's black?

CAROL: Come on, Neecy. Tell them.

WANDA: Tell us what?

NEECY: Jadah's grandmother is a Melville, she's sister to our Nana Therese.

MARGIE: What?

CAROL: She was taken to the Cootamundra Girls Home.

NEECY: When her mother died, her auntie found her and brought her back home.

CAROL: Nana Therese!

MARGIE: Who did Nana Therese get married to again?

NEECY: Bunna!

MARGIE: That's right! Bunna!

NEECY: Kitty had Nana Therese.

CAROL: She had two husbands. The first one died.

WANDA: She had five kids.

NEECY: No, no, no. She had six.

MARGIE: Three to her first husband …

CAROL: … and three to the second.

NEECY: They also took in Auntie Mavis's daughter.

WANDA: That's where the Mitchell name comes in.

CAROL: He was a whitefulla.

NEECY: Come in for the shearing.

CAROL: Her first husband was a blackfella.

NEECY: Jadah's dad's grandfather.

CAROL: One of the Nurra boys!

MARGIE: Related to the Jacksons.

CAROL: That's right.

NEECY: Jadah's dad is Paul Nurra.

WANDA: He's brother to Kevin …

MARGIE: Oh, Kevin!

WANDA: … and his other two brothers …

CAROL: … Vincent …

NEECY: … and Lance.

MARGIE: Lance who married Amy.

NEECY: No. No. No. That's Lance Senior.

CAROL: Lance Junior married Glennys Atkins.

NEECY: They named their little boy after Paul.

WANDA: Paul Nurra.

NEECY: Jadah's dad.

CAROL: Our nana and his grandmother were half sisters.

NEECY: So that makes Jadah our cousin.

> *Pause.*

WANDA: Well, I don't give a stuff who she's related to! Who does she think she is anyway?! Putting our flag on her mootcha!

CHANTELLE: It's art, Auntie Wanda!

WANDA: Art!

CAROL: I think she's making a statement about her identity.

WANDA: You can't be brought up white and rock up to any old community and call yourself one of us.

NEECY: Jadah is as black as you and me.

WANDA: She's not a blackfella! She just wants a cheap housing loan!

SCENE THIRTEEN

JADAH *storms into the camp, drenched from head to toe.*

JADAH: Fuck you! You're worse than the assimilationists! You want me to disappear! Well, I won't! I'm right here!

I know who I am! My father, my grandmother, my aunties and cousins. In those photos! That is who I am! That's my family. Not you! [*Pointing to* WANDA] Or anyone like you!

JADAH *dries herself off and puts her clothes on.*

WANDA: Don't you point your finger at me! You just want blackfella 'benefits'!

JADAH: What 'benefit' is there in being accused of being a fake?! I'm sick of having to prove myself to everyone! It's fucking exhausting!

WANDA: Yeah, must be real tiring having to turn your blackness on and off all day.

CAROL: Our culture is about kinship, not colour.

WANDA: What would you know. Ms 'Flashblack I've Got A Job In The City', with ya dyed hair and manicured nails, working for that Gubbar Institution?!

CAROL: What's wrong with manicured nails?!

WANDA: With your inner-city apartment and brand new car and PhD thesis! You think you're shit hot!

CAROL: Yeah, come on …

She starts to square up to WANDA.

MARGIE: Calm down, ladies.

CHANTELLE: Fight! Fight!

NEECY: For Christ's sake!

WANDA: What would you know about living in community?! What would you know, sitting in some air-conditioned fucking office?! You can't go to the milk bar around here to buy the kids an icy pole without everybody's white beady eyes looking at you! We're living it, sister! Right here!

CAROL: Just because I'm not scratching around in the dirt trying to feed myself with my arse hanging out of my pants, I'm not a blackfella?!

WANDA: No, Carol! I'm saying you're a coconut!

The women hold CAROL *back.*

Which is worse than this one here! [*Pointing to* JADAH] Who shouldn't be calling herself a blackfella in the first place!

JADAH: Why don't you hand us some 'dog tags' while you're at it?!

JADAH *starts to pack up her bags.*

CAROL: If you're so worried about people with white skin, maybe you should get some better contraception, because I've seen some white fullas sniffing around your house like dogs on heat!

WANDA: How dare you bring my kids into this?!

NEECY: That's enough!

CAROL: You started it! Two of your kids were fathered by white men!

MARGIE: What's wrong with having a white partner?!

WANDA: Shut up!

NEECY: I said, that's enough!

WANDA: You've never had a boyfriend in your life. Black or white!

MARGIE: As a matter of fact I do have a partner and *she's white*!

WANDA: What?!

MARGIE: You heard me!

NEECY: We've said enough!

WANDA: You have the hide to criticise my life!

NEECY: Stop it! Just stop!

> *The women back down.* JADAH *has packed her bag and goes to leave the camp.*

Jadah, stay here! It's too dark to drive out of here now.

> JADAH *hesitates.*

Come on, Jadah. Stay here the night. Stay.

> *One by one the women put their plates away and put themselves to bed.* MARGIE *moves her bed away from* WANDA *and goes to move the big cardboard box.*

Leave that box there!

MARGIE: I'm not sleeping next to Wanda.

NEECY: The box stays here with me.

SCENE FOURTEEN

All of the women are in bed except for CAROL *and* CHANTELLE *who's on her bed listening to music.* CAROL *puts on a face mask and hairnet, shines a torch on her bed, shakes her pillows and doona loudly, checks in her pyjamas, fluffs her pillows and takes forever to get to bed.*

NEECY: Carol! Will you stop rustling around!

WANDA: We're trying to get some sleep here.

CAROL: Can someone please check my bed in case a snake has crawled in there?

NEECY: Chantelle! Check ya auntie's bed, for Christ's sake! Then we can get some sleep.

> CHANTELLE *shines a torch in* CAROL*'s bed.*

CHANTELLE: No snakes, Auntie Carol.

> CHANTELLE *sees Jadah's phone on her bag, grabs it and starts wandering out of camp.*

NEECY: Chantelle!

CHANTELLE: What?!

NEECY: Where do you think you're going?

CHANTELLE: I'm just going to the djillowar!

NEECY: Uh-uh! Not on my watch. You're not leaving this camp at night.

CHANTELLE: I'm busting!

NEECY: I don't care! You shoulda gone when it was daylight.

> CHANTELLE *continues to walk off but is then stopped in her tracks.*

Margie, tell Ms Smartypants here, about the hairy bekka.

CHANTELLE: I've heard it a million times.

MARGIE: That hairy bekka, she's one big, hairy, scary woman. She lives in the rivers. In the deep waterholes and scurries quickly across the land.

WANDA: You can tell where she is in the water. There'll be bubbles and there'll be a whirlpool.

MARGIE: Don't go swimming in the river where the water is rough and don't go walking around the bush on your own at night. That's where the hairy bekka is and she'll grab you by the foot and she'll gobble you up and spit your bones out!

WANDA: That hairy bekka, she's a short, wrinkly old woman with the longest arms you'll ever see …

MARGIE: And long, dry, wrinkled-up tits that hit her knees when she runs! Her hair is so long and grey, it drags on the ground behind her.

CHANTELLE: That story doesn't scare me.

WANDA: Little kids have been known to find strands of the hairy bekka's hair on the bushes.

MARGIE: And she wears a giant dillybag on her back where she puts the little ones she's taken for her dinner.

WANDA: And she runs with them little legs through the bush. Like lightning.

MARGIE: Like a flash! One minute she's there, then she's gone.

WANDA: And the little kids, they be screaming! Screaming out for their mothers, but no-one can hear.

MARGIE: Only the hairy bekka with the little children in her dillybag and when the children cry out for their mothers she'll fling one of her long, dry teats over her shoulder and try to put it in the children's mouth to stop them from crying.

ALL: Ewwwwww!

WANDA: You smell her before you see her!

MARGIE: But she never takes any kids from camp.

NEECY: Only when they've been naughty. Or wandered off at night. Isn't that right, Chantelle?

CHANTELLE: Whatever!

MARGIE: And that's the truth.

> CHANTELLE *humpfs back to bed.*
>
> *Lights out.*

SCENE FIFTEEN

The women are fast asleep and JADAH *stirs restlessly. She has entered the dreaming.*

The women rise up out of their beds, transformed as spirits of the old ones. They wear furs, headbands, old torn dresses, their faces obscured. Deep black eyes. Long grey and black hair. They circle Jadah's bed, whispering to her in a barely discernible language, overlapping and repeating phrases.

VARIOUS WOMEN: *Ngani deyawin wamayirr* [Who is this one woman?]
    Dhadhiwa deyawin [Still a little girl, this one]
    Ganbina! Ganbina! [Wake up! Wake up!]
    Baparra banarrak ngina birrama [Long time now, you've been gone]
    Minhe ngina itjumutj [What makes you sick?]

> *The language becomes more pronounced, more urgent, incessant, almost violent as the old ones try to get* JADAH *to see.*

Birratj! Gaka! [Quick! Come on!]
Ganbina! Ganbina! [Wake up! Wake up!]
Nyinyindhan ngani narrak [Who are you fighting?]
Nyuandanan lupa dhama yenbena [You gotta carry us old people]
ALL: [*together*] *Damnanan ngarri* [Tell them]
Lotjpa! Lotjpa! [Speak! Speak!]
Damnanan ngarri [Tell them]
Lotjpa! [Speak!]
Ganbina! [Wake up!]

> JADAH *wakes in fright and the women slide back to their beds.*
> NEECY *comforts* JADAH.

NEECY: Jadah.
JADAH: I couldn't move!
NEECY: It's alright.
JADAH: I was stuck there.
NEECY: Come on now.
JADAH: They were talking to me and talking to me, but nothing was coming out.
NEECY: You're safe now.
JADAH: I didn't have any words.
NEECY: You know, darlin', if you're having strong dreams, that's okay. That's just the old ones trying to tell you something. They wake us up! There's nothing to fear out here. That river there? That's one blood. One river.

> *She looks to the river.*

This here. This is your grandmother's country. This is your country.
I see you. I see who you are.
Can you feel it, darling? It's all around us. Under your feet. In your heartbeat. In the ground and way up in the sky.
Your grandmother told me your story, time and time again.
Remember that song your nan used to sing?
JADAH: Yeah.
JADAH and NEECY: [*singing together*] *Ngal-nya woka ngana-buraya moya moya moya*
Ngal-nya woka ngana-buraya moya moya moya
[There is a happy land, far far away]

NEECY: You don't have to prove nothing to nobody.

It's all here. In ya blood.

In this country.

JADAH: Why didn't you tell them who I was?

NEECY: Wanda and Margie?

JADAH: Yeah.

NEECY: Coming home isn't always easy. You gotta find your own way.

NEECY *leads* JADAH *back to her bed.*

SCENE SIXTEEN

It's late at night and CHANTELLE *has wandered deep into the bush with Jadah's phone. She waits and waits for her boyfriend to pick up the call. The phone rings out and she tries again. Finally she gets through.*

CHANTELLE: Hello … Hello … Hey … Is that you? What? It's Chantelle! Hey, babe!

I can't hear you! Turn the music down. I said, turn the music down!

What?! What do you mean you can't talk? No! Don't hang up. I wanna hear your voice. Go into the other room!

Why didn't you text me back?

I told you! I get paid on Tuesday. I haven't got any money!

No, no, no, no, don't hang up! I'll get us some money as soon as I can.

What?!

Alright! Alright! I've got twenty bucks, but you have to come and pick me up.

Tonight?!

Okay. I'll meet you at the crossroads.

You've gotta drive to Picola and turn left at the post office. The sign's a bit faded, so look out for it. Take a left, go down about twelve k until you see a big red letterbox at the end of a farmer's driveway, take a left at the track opposite the driveway.

Go down there, then you gotta take a turn right about ten k's down, then left at the fork, then left, then left again. I'll be there at the crossroads. Got it?

I miss you, babe. Do you miss me?

Pause.

She hangs up the phone. She is lost.

SCENE SEVENTEEN

JADAH *sits up from her swag and looks at the glorious sunrise. She lets it heal her. She gets up, grabs her camera and takes a few photos.*

WANDA *wakes, gets out of her swag and sits at the fire. She watches* JADAH *take photos.*

WANDA: Come out here to make some art out of us, have ya? Show all your international art dealers some *real* blackfellas.

Here we are! All out here. 'Ooga booga'-ring on country! In fact, there's a real good name for your next show—'Ooga Booga'!

You'd sell those pictures for quite a lot, hey? How much money do you make for ya 'pitchas', huh?! Two thousand? Ten thousand? Twenty thousand? Hmm?

Gonna sell off our images to the highest bidder? [*Feigning a foreign art buyer*] 'Oh look, Pierre! Look at those Real Aborigines she's captured. I can see the interplay between light and shadow and the way the image juxtaposes with the rusty car in the background. Pass me my Mastercard.'

You make art for white people!

You didn't come out here for Neecy. You came out here for your own fucked-up career ambitions. At the end of the day, your 'art' is gonna end up in some penthouse apartment so dinner guests can wank off and have polite dinner conversation about the 'Aboriginal problem'.

Here!

She stands up and makes a Black Panther pose.

Here's some *art*! Take a photo of this?!

JADAH: Who the fuck are you anyway?!

WANDA: I'm a single mother with five kids whose been dispossessed of her land and is living off a pittance and now they wanna go put us on the BasicsCard so that I can queue up at the redneck supermarket and buy limp lettuce for five dollars a pop! Go on! Take a photo of this? I dare ya!

Angeline Penrith as Wanda in the Moogahlin Performing Arts production in 2016. (Photo: Michele Mossop)

WANDA *pushes her face into* JADAH*'s.* JADAH *does not back down. She takes a step back from* WANDA *and brings her camera up.*

I fucking dare ya?!

JADAH *clicks the camera button.*

Put *that* in ya fucking art gallery!

WANDA *sits back down at the fire.* JADAH *puts her camera away.*

SCENE EIGHTEEN

One by one the women wake in their swags and look to the perfect sunrise. CAROL *wakes with a start.*

CAROL: I had the strangest dream. I was in this big open space. Like a field, or a sand dune or something. Like a big … I dunno. There was a horizon. This thin red line thing that was pulsating, like this … And I'm walking on this ground. Like it's hard and then it went soft and then it went crunchy. And I'm walking on … like this carpet of gum leaves. I'm walking and all this … this beautiful smell of eucalyptus was coming up and into my nose. Like I could see it! And into my chest and I'm breathing it in and breathing it in. And then I come to this like river. But it wasn't a river, it was like this black, shiny … I dunno, it was moving … And then suddenly there's this woman. This old woman. Tribal. Sitting crossed-legged in front of me. Just looking at me with these deep black eyes. And she's got these scars … Here and here … White-grey hair and these big whiskers on her chin and she was singing and motioning towards me. Like this. And then …

     … she just got up and started drinking from this can of Coke Zero … with a straw!

WANDA: What?!

CAROL: I dunno! I musta been thirsty. What's for breakfast?

MARGIE: I was thinking of cooking us a continental breakfast. French toast with cinnamon and maple syrup.

WANDA: Now ya talking. And bacon.

MARGIE: Yeah and French pastries.

CAROL: Have we got real coffee?

WANDA: What do ya mean have we got *real* coffee?

MARGIE: Check out Neecy!

CAROL: She must need the sleep!

MARGIE: She's holding onto that box as if it's her man!

The women laugh loudly and wake NEECY *up.*

CAROL: Morning, Neecy.

NEECY: Bloody hell, Carol! You let me sleep in!

CAROL: We were just dreaming up some French toast with maple syrup and freshly brewed coffee.

NEECY: We've got business to do today.

She leaps out of bed.

Gotta get some gum leaves together!

Jadah, get your camera.

CAROL: Have breakfast first.

NEECY: You should've woken me up.

She notices Chantelle's bed is empty.

Where's Chantelle?

CAROL: I dunno.

NEECY: Did anyone see Chantelle go?

WANDA: Not me.

JADAH: [*noticing her phone is missing*] Neecy, my phone's gone!

NEECY: I told her not to use that phone!

MARGIE: She was asking me about how to get out of here yesterday.

NEECY: [*yelling out*] Chantelle! Did anyone see her in her bed this morning when you woke up?

JADAH: No, come to think of it.

NEECY: Who was up first this morning?

JADAH: Me!

WANDA: She can't have gone that far!

NEECY: Don't you bet on it.

CAROL: She might've just gone for a morning walk.

NEECY: She never gets up this early. Wanda and Margie, you look that way. Jadah, and Carol, you look over there.

CAROL, MARGIE, WANDA *and* JADAH *all exit as they call out Chantelle's name.*

SCENE NINETEEN [A]

MARGIE *and* WANDA *are searching for Chantelle.* WANDA *has her GPS tracking device out.*

WANDA: Bloody hell, Margie! Will you give that thing a rest!

MARGIE: I'm just taking a few co-ordinates so that we can find our way back.

WANDA: The old uncles never needed a GPS when they were out tracking.

MARGIE: Let's go this way.

WANDA: Margie, will you stop waving that stupid GPS thing everywhere!

MARGIE: Karen showed me how to use it so we never get stranded in the bush.

WANDA: Karen, Karen, Karen!

MARGIE: Hey, I've never judged you!

WANDA: It's not about your girlfriend!

MARGIE: Don't you want me to be happy?

WANDA: I tell you everything! I told you about when I went for that job and didn't get it. I told you when I had that affair. I told you about that time I got pregnant and I didn't want Mum to know. I tell you when I'm scared. I tell you everything!

MARGIE: Why would I tell you?! You make it impossible!

WANDA: And you know what hurts the most? That you told everybody else about your girlfriend before you told me. I'm your big sister!

MARGIE: You're so angry all of the time. It scares people. You've gotta forgive once in a while.

WANDA: Shut ya face, Margie!

MARGIE: See! This is what you do!

SCENE NINETEEN [B]

CAROL *and* JADAH *are in the bush searching for Chantelle.*

CAROL: Chantelle!

JADAH: I should never have given her that phone in the first place.

CAROL: She would've taken off anyway. Chantelle!

JADAH: Looking for that man of hers?

CAROL: Dickhead. Ice addict.

JADAH: Ice? Shit.

CAROL: I'm sorry about Wanda.

JADAH: You don't have to apologise for Wanda.

CAROL: I get it.

JADAH: You get what?

CAROL: I think what you're doing with your art is great.

JADAH: Really?

CAROL: Yes!

JADAH: You don't think it's too much?

CAROL: No. They hate it! Those bigots! You stir them up. You make some of us blackfellas squirm too.

JADAH: You don't think it's too full-on?

CAROL: No. Go on, exhibit it.

JADAH: I get sick of everyone telling me I'm not black.

CAROL: It's brave.

JADAH: What you've done for Neecy … that's brave.

SCENE NINETEEN [C]

MARGIE *and* WANDA.

MARGIE: If you're so great at telling me about everything all of the time, why didn't you tell me that dickhead excuse of a man of yours has been hitting you?!

WANDA: No he hasn't!

MARGIE: I've seen the bruises.

WANDA: It wasn't him.

MARGIE: Wanda, I've seen the bruises. More than once!

WANDA: It wasn't him!

MARGIE: Look at where we are, Wanda? Look at this. [*Looking out to country*] There's beautiful country everywhere.

WANDA: Oh, for fuck's sake!

WANDA *exits, looking for Chantelle.* MARGIE *follows her.*

SCENE NINETEEN [D]

CAROL *and* JADAH.

JADAH: Chantelle!

CAROL: Chantelle!

JADAH: I don't know what the hell I'm doing here.

CAROL: You're on your grandmother's country.

JADAH: I used to dream about this place all the time. I didn't think it'd be like this!

CAROL: She was a beautiful woman, your nan.

JADAH: Yeah. She was sad too.

CAROL : She was from the stolen gen, bub.

JADAH: I know. [*Shouting*] Fuck them! How could they do that to a little girl! Fuck them for doing that to her!

CAROL: Yeah.

JADAH: It makes me want to scream!

CAROL: Yeah, fuck them!

JADAH: Fuck them!

CAROL *and* JADAH *have fun with their echo.*

CAROL and JADAH: [*together*] Fuck them, fuck them, fuck them …

CAROL: You just keep making your art, sister.

JADAH: Chantelle!

SCENE NINETEEN [*E*]

MARGIE *is marching after* WANDA *in the bush.*

MARGIE: … Yeah well, if this man's such a great bloke, why the fuck has he got 'prison' as his occupation on his Facebook page?!

WANDA: What?! You're his Facebook friend?!

MARGIE: And if you're so big on telling me everything, why didn't you tell me he just got out of gaol? Again!

WANDA: Because it's none of your business!

MARGIE: 'Occupation: Gaol'. On his Facebook page! I had to show Karen. Like, you can't make this shit up!

WANDA: What's he doing liking you on Facebook anyway?!

MARGIE: He's a waste of space, he's dealing drugs and he's dragging you down with him.

WANDA: Fuck you!

MARGIE: No! Fuck you! Get your shit together. Stop bringing these idiot men into your home. It's your kids' home, not theirs, and you deserve the best!

WANDA: Why the fuck do you think I've come out here!?

MARGIE: Come and stay at my place with the kids until the dickhead moves out.

WANDA: What about you and Karen?

MARGIE: What do you mean?

WANDA: What will I tell the kids?

MARGIE: For fuck sake!

> MARGIE *exits,* WANDA *follows.*

SCENE NINETEEN [F]

NEECY *is waiting at the camp.*

NEECY: Chantelle!

> Bloody Chantelle! I could throttle her! And her bloody mother! Chantelle!
>
> Where was Chantelle's mother when she won the netball finals? Huh? Where was she when she went to the debutante ball?
>
> Where was she when little Chantelle got her first period? Where is she now?! Locked up! That's where!?
>
> Chantelle! Where are you? Chantelle!
>
> She's too little to have a baby.
>
> Come back home, Chantelle.
>
> My little Woman of the Sun.
>
> Come home, my darling.
>
> Come home.

SCENE TWENTY

CAROL *and* JADAH *enter the camp.*

JADAH: Neecy, we found my phone on the track about a mile off.

CAROL: She must've dropped it.

NEECY: Shit!

CAROL: We've looked everywhere.

> WANDA *and* MARGIE *enter.*

MARGIE: Sorry, Neecy, my co-ordinates are out!

JADAH: I shouldn't have given her that phone in the first place.

WANDA: Where were you born? Under a rock?

NEECY: Margie and Jadah, you drive into town. Wanda and Carol, you keep looking.

CAROL: I'm not going out there with her!

NEECY: I don't give a stuff!

JADAH: We'll report her missing to the cops!

WANDA: Yeah, as if they'll get off their arses and start searching straight away. Young black kids go missing all the time. They don't give a stuff!

CAROL: We've gotta let someone know.

JADAH: The SES.

WANDA: The SES!

CAROL: This is an emergency.

NEECY: We've lost Chantelle.

WANDA: We've lost Chantelle! You lost her!

NEECY: Yes, I lost her! I fucking lost her, alright! She's lost! What the hell was I thinking?! Bringing you all out here! You and Margie are at each other's throats! Carol's gonna lose her job. And poor Jadah! I'm sorry for bringing you out here. I don't know what the hell I'm doing out here.

I keep calling out and calling out to the ancestors, but no-one is answering me back!

She calls out to the old ones.

Tell me what the fuck do to?!

The women stand in stunned silence. NEECY *waits for a sign.*

I can't do this. Come on, everyone. Let's go.

NEECY *starts packing up all of the gear.*

MARGIE: Neecy?

NEECY: Come on, Carol. Pack up. Let's get out of here.

WANDA: This is bullshit! Where are the keys?

WANDA *starts packing up too.*

NEECY: Yes! Great! Let's all go.

CAROL: Neecy, we can't.

NEECY: Yes we can. Come on, let's get the hell out of here. Come on. Pack up!

CHANTELLE *wanders back into camp, sits on her bed, puts her headphones in her ears and rocks her head to the beat of the music as if nothing happened.*

The women notice CHANTELLE *on the bed.*

Silence.

CAROL: Neecy.

MARGIE: Neecy.

CAROL: Look what the cat dragged in!

Silence.

CHANTELLE *ignores the women and continues to listen to the music.*

NEECY: Chantelle! Where the hell have you been?

CHANTELLE: What did you say?

NEECY *drags* CHANTELLE *off the bed, rips the headphones out of her ears and goes to give her a good flogging, but* CHANTELLE *gets away.*

NEECY: Don't you ever ever walk away from camp again! Have you got that?! Are you listening to me girl?! What the hell is wrong with you?!

CHANTELLE: Nothing!

CAROL: You frightened the living daylights out of us!

CHANTELLE: I went to make a phone call!

NEECY: In the middle of the bloody night!

CHANTELLE: I didn't even wanna come on this poxy camping trip!

NEECY: I brought you out here for some culture.

CHANTELLE: Culture! Fuck ya culture!

NEECY: Have some respect!

CAROL: Don't you talk to your auntie like that!

WANDA: Chantelle, apologise to your Auntie Neecy please.

CHANTELLE: I just wanna be with my boyfriend!

NEECY: Chantelle, you've got your whole life ahead of you, girl.

CHANTELLE: My whole life ahead of me? What life? There's no jobs in town for girls like me. My teacher doesn't even try. She's already got me in the dole queue. And have a look at yourselves! Look at you all! Youse haven't stopped arguing since you got here!

Beat. The women exchange looks.

You call this culture?! This one here [*pointing to* CAROL] hates her fucking job and is desperate for a root.

WANDA: Watch your language!

CAROL: I'm not desperate!

CHANTELLE: This one here [*pointing to* WANDA] is jealous of that one there [*pointing to* CAROL]. This one here [*pointing to* JADAH] doesn't know whether she's black or white! And this one here [*pointing to* MARGIE] is in the closet! Auntie Margie, we *all* knew you were gay years ago—

MARGIE: Really?

CHANTELLE: I've got a gay-dar, you know. Stop hiding.

And you! [*Pointing to* NEECY] You will never be my mother! No matter how hard you try! I *hate* her! I hate my mother's fucking drug-fucked guts! It's fucked! I'm fat, I'm ugly and I'm black!

MARGIE: You're not ugly, darling …

CAROL: Or fat!

WANDA: Black is beautiful.

CHANTELLE: And I keep going back! Even when he grabs my arm real tight, or puts his hand around my throat for a game. For a laugh. And then he hits me and tells me he loves me. 'Come on, baby. Have a bong, baby. I'm gonna buy you a ring, baby!' And I keep coming back.

He said he was gonna meet me at the crossroads.

And I'm sitting there in the pitch black with nothing but one fucking mopoke to keep me company. Not a star in the sky.

And then I felt it coming.

Down there.

Warm and slow.

I thought I was gonna have a baby. I really wanted to have a baby. Give me something to do. To be.

Auntie Wanda. Take me home.

WANDA: No, darling.

CHANTELLE: Let's go.

WANDA: I know where that ends up.

CHANTELLE: I wanna go home!

WANDA: The hitting.

CHANTELLE: He told me he loved me.

WANDA: We're not going anywhere. We're staying right here.

Pause.

NEECY: Carol. Get that box and bring it over here.

CAROL *nods and brings the box to* NEECY.

SCENE TWENTY-ONE

CAROL *carefully opens the lid of the box and lifts up a resplendent possum-skin cloak.*

NEECY: This cloak belonged to Towradgi. All of us here, she is our great-great-great-grandmother.

Many women made this cloak. Winyanboga. Many women like me and like you. They scraped with mussel shell and they sewed with the kangaroo sinew. They prepared and softened the skins by the fire. They chatted. Stories and gossip and bloodlines. Many a marriage arranged around this cloak.

NEECY *gestures towards* CAROL *who places the cloak carefully around* NEECY*'s shoulders.*

The museum call this the 'Maiden's Punt cloak', but Towradgi, she was no maiden, she was a lore woman. A lore enforcer. A resistance fighter. She waved her stick at the white men and they looked at her stupidly. 'What's this old woman saying? Look at her with her teeth missing and her saggy, wrinkled tits.'

But Towradgi, she sprayed her language at them! She swore and she cursed! She pointed her boney finger. She raised her *winyarrin nanyirr* to these men. Right here. At this sacred site. She died protecting us.

This isn't the 'Maiden's Punt cloak'. We call this 'Towradgi's cloak'. Tell them that at the museum, Carol.

CAROL: Yes, Neecy. I will.

NEECY: You are the guardian of this cloak.

CAROL: Yes, Neecy.

NEECY: Now bring everything else out. Carefully now.

CAROL *puts on some white curator's gloves and hands the arte-facts to the women.*

WANDA: Where did you get these?

NEECY: Carol's work.

CAROL: Things go missing all the time in those places, don't they, Neecy?

NEECY: Bad record-keeping too.

> CAROL *hands a basket to* MARGIE.

Margie. That's your nan's basket.

MARGIE: [*holding it gently*] Now *that's* how you weave a basket!

WANDA: Look how tight she's got that stitch.

NEECY: Look how she tails off the ending.

> CAROL *brings out an emu feather skirt.*

Chantelle? I want you to wear this.

> NEECY *and* CAROL *put the emu feather skirt around* CHANTELLE'*s waist.*

Now give Chantelle your artefacts.

> *Each woman dresses* CHANTELLE *with the objects, it's a clunky initiation.*

MARGIE: [*tying a headband around* CHANTELLE'*s head*] Here ya go, sis.

JADAH: [*putting a necklace over* CHANTELLE'*s head*] With reeds from this very river …

WANDA: [*handing her the basket*] That's how you weave a basket.

NEECY: [*handing* CHANTELLE *her digging stick*] You're gonna need this to keep them boys under control.

> CHANTELLE *stands replete and beautiful in full dress. The women admire her.* NEECY *takes the ochre from the coolamon* CAROL *is holding and puts it on* CHANTELLE'*s face.*

This is your grandmother's country.

> *She puts ochre on all of the women's faces, saving* CAROL *until last.*

You are Koori women. Koori women from the Yorta Yorta mob. We are Winyanboga Yurringa and this is our country.

> *She finally reaches* CAROL, *putting ochre on her face.*

Thank you, Carol.

> *The women finally stand in silence for a moment. They are listening to country. They look to* CHANTELLE.

WANDA: You look beautiful, Chantelle.

JADAH: You look deadly, sis!

JADAH takes photos of CHANTELLE *and the women.*

NEECY: *Winyanboga* [Many women]
Winyanboga Yurringa [Women, Sun]
My Women of the Sun
It's time to give the artefacts back.

The women take the artefacts off CHANTELLE *and go to put them in the box.*

Not there.

She points to the hole in the sand that she dug at the beginning of the play.

Here.

The women look to NEECY *nervously. One by one they decide to lay their artefacts into the ground.* NEECY *kneels on the ground and slowly covers the artefacts with earth.*

Show me the way.

The women join her and one by one they too cover the artefacts.

MARGIE: Which way to go.

CHANTELLE: How to be.

JADAH: Here.

CAROL: In this place.

JADAH: Here.

WANDA: Sad and happy.

MARGIE: All at once.

CHANTELLE: I fear you.

NEECY: I love you.

JADAH: I have searched for you.

WANDA: Our people.

CAROL: Our song.

CHANTELLE: Our dance.

MARGIE: Our country.

NEECY: Here.

The repatriation is complete. The women place their hands on the mound and NEECY *invites them to stand.*

NEECY *motions to* JADAH. *It's time for her to sing her nan's song.*
JADAH *sings and the women join her.*

JADAH: [*singing*] *Ngal-nya woka ngana-buraya moya moya moya*
ALL: [*singing together*] *Ngal-nya woka ngana-buraya moya moya moya*
Ngal-nya woka ngana-buraya moya moya moya
[There is a happy land, far far away]

NEECY *hands the women bunches of gum leaves and they smoke and cleanse the country.*

They sing and dance their love into the earth.

Lights slowly fade.

THE END